The Invaluable Assistant

The Invaluable Assistant

30+ Ways to Prove Your Value at Work

Sandy Geroux, M.S.

WOWplace International, LLC/Wesley Chapel, FL

Sandy Geroux/**WOWplace** International, LLC

Wesley Chapel, FL

www.the**WOWplace**.com

For general information about our other products and services, please contact Sandy Geroux at (407) 856-1188 or sandy@the**WOWplace**.com.

The Invaluable Assistant/Sandy Geroux -- 1st ed.

978-0-9788269-8-7

This book is dedicated to all the hardworking administrative professionals who keep our leaders organized and our organizations running smoothly.

Thank you for all you do every day.

Table of Contents

Introduction

Most administrative assistants I know are hard-working professionals whose work is often undervalued and contributions frequently underestimated. Some are in this profession for a short time, while others choose to make it their lifelong career. No matter how long they stay, all serve as the backbone of their organization every day as they help their leaders become more efficient, effective and organized. In addition to their ordinary, defined duties, they are often also asked to lead teams, plan events and take on a multitude of tasks they've never done before, in the hopes that they can accomplish the "impossible."

In the past, most have done it with precious little training or support, finding their way and creating success virtually on their own.

Fortunately, this has changed, as there are now many conferences, held all around the world, specifically geared toward these professionals. EAs, PAs, entry-level assistants, administrative managers and directors and more are now gathering to share their knowledge and help each other succeed. In fact, there are at least 145 different job titles that fall under the administrative professional heading. All are welcome at these events.

Most occupants of these positions (approximately 95%) are women, but that is also beginning to change as men are starting to realize the personal satisfaction of serving in the role of a true executive partner to the leaders of their organizations.

I have over 20 years of personal experience as an administrative professional, having begun as a receptionist in a medical office and working my way up through the ranks over the years to serve several CEOs of multi-national companies in the process.

I enjoyed my time in all of these positions. They allowed me to learn a lot about people, and business… and even offered me the opportunity to dip my toe into technology – and then dive in head-first by becoming a Business Systems Consultant/Systems Analyst. I subsequently owned my own desktop publishing business before laptops and smartphones became commonplace.

Since leaving the corporate environment, I have been a small business owner for many years, and have spent the last 20 years training others, thousands of whom are administrative professionals.

My love for the changes in the profession over the years, as well as my respect for these incredibly resilient professionals, are boundless. Although I serve as instructor and coach for many, they have all taught me countless lessons along the way that I will never forget.

In an effort to gather and offer as much knowledge as possible to them, I conducted a research study and asked a multitude of leaders what they value most in their assistants.

This book was created from that research, and it contains tips and ideas for moving yourself from being **indispensable** to becoming **invaluable** to your leaders, your teams and your entire organization. Stories accompany many of the ideas so you can see them applied in real life. None of these ideas and tips are fluff or theory. They are all based on real-world experience, most in the actual words of the leaders I interviewed.

As you read the book, the significant difference in the two terms "indispensable" and "invaluable" will become apparent. After reading the concept and the story that illustrates it, I hope you will never again deem yourself to be merely indispensable, but will move yourself, through these ideas and many of your own, to become truly *invaluable* in your role in any organization.

Here's to your successful career!

Chapter One:

Indispensable vs. Invaluable

Indispensable vs. Invaluable

When many assistants think about their contributions and value to their organization, they traditionally consider themselves indispensable.

While this may be true on some level, if you really think about it, the true goal should not be "indispensable" but "invaluable." Many people (and some dictionaries!) use these terms interchangeably, but they are really not interchangeable at all in the context of people in business.

The following story illustrates the significant difference between these two terms and the mindsets that accompany them.

You're the one that I want

A friend of mine related this story from his time as a Training Director back in the 1980s. His company had merged with another company, causing the unfortunate situation where there were two employees for many positions that only needed one. The Training Director position was one of them.

The CEO had to decide which employee in each position would stay and which would be let go. He prepared his presentation for the Board of Directors and asked his assistant to type it up and prepare slides for his presentation.

But you must remember that at that time, there was no PowerPoint, no laptops, no LCD projector. This task has to be accomplished on a typewriter, with the typed pages being brought to the Training Department because they had the equipment to transfer those pages onto transparent sheets (called "transparencies") so they could be put onto an overhead projector and shown during his presentation to the Board.

As an aside for those of you who don't know what an overhead projector is, it's a piece of equipment that had a glass top, on which the transparency was placed. A light bulb under the glass shone through the transparency and a lens and projector projected the image on the transparency onto a screen. This was an amazing piece of technology, except when you turned it on and the bulb blew out (which happened frequently!) and it took 20 minutes to replace it before you could use the projector!

Back to the story: So, the CEO's assistant brought the typed presentation deck to the Training Department and asked my friend, the Training Director, to make the transparencies. While doing so, he saw *his own name* on the list of people to be cut! Talk about a lack of data security!

With two choices at that point (either say nothing or storm down to the CEO's office and demand an explanation), he wisely chose the former while he decided what to do.

He remembered that about a year prior, he had helped the CEO with an important project that required unique and uncommon knowledge and skills that he possessed. In fact, his skills were so advanced that he not only trained the two gentlemen hired for the project but he helped the CEO interview candidates and decide who to hire. He also knew that those gentlemen were doing great.

So, he waited a day or two until he saw the CEO in the hallway, when he subtly dropped the question, *"How are those two guys working out for you?"*

The CEO answered, *"Great! Thank you so much for your help in getting and training them!"*

Boom! What did he do? He reminded the CEO of the unique added value he had brought to the table that not many other training directors possessed.

When the CEO made his final list, he gave it to his assistant to type up and she brought it to the Training Department. My friend was thrilled to see that his name was no longer on the list! The *other* training director had been cut!

The focus was no longer on the general tasks outlined in the job description. Instead, the focus had switched to the specific added value that one candidate brought to the table over the other.

The critical point that this story illustrates is that the *position* was indispensable. Someone needed to fill that position. However, the *person* selected to fill it was the one who was invaluable to the team, who possessed additional skills, experience or talents that the other candidate did not.

Who brought more to the table? Who benefited the organization more? What talents does the selected candidate possess that most others do not? These were the questions considered when making the final decision of who would be offered the position.

This is an important revelation! The focus was no longer on the general tasks outlined in the job description. Instead, the focus had switched to the specific *added* value that one candidate brought to the table over the other.

Indispensable

in·dis·pen·sa·ble /ində'spensəb(ə)l ~ adjective: absolutely necessary.

When you're viewed as indispensable, what happens? Your *presence* is absolutely necessary, either in person, by phone or virtually. You can't take a day off. You can't get sick. You can't be out of communication for any length of time.

Why? Because the focus is on the specific TASKS that you do. But if the only focus is on the tasks that need to be done, many people can fill that role. Just get somebody – anybody – in there and have them "push the right buttons" and get the tasks done.

When you are viewed as merely indispensable, *anyone* will do. You become a commodity, the formal definition of which is *"an article of trade or commerce, esp. a product as distinguished from a service; something of use, advantage, or value... able to be traded away for something else."*

Since you can easily trade one commodity for another, no one wants to pay more for it. With commodities, the focus is on cost – they're all pretty much the same, so just get it the cheapest, quickest and easiest you can. And if you lose one, just replace it with another.

In the context of this discussion, if you simply substitute the word "person" for "product," you realize that anyone who doesn't distinguish themselves for any particular reason could be viewed as not unique, invaluable, or distinguishable from everyone (or anyone) else. Therefore, there's no need to insist on hiring or retaining that person. If you are a seasoned professional and you want to add extra insurance against being replaced by a less experienced, less costly person, don't be a commodity!

Become an asset instead! An asset is defined as a useful and desirable quality or thing (in this case, a person).

When you become an asset, you move from being indispensable (where *anyone* will do) to being truly invaluable, where *no one else* will do because the organization can't easily replace your knowledge, expertise, work ethic, thoroughness, thoughtfulness – or a million other factors that make you so valuable (invaluable).

Invaluable

in·val·u·a·ble /in'valy(oo)əb(ə)l/ ~ adjective: beyond calculable or appraisable value; of inestimable worth; priceless.

Why do certain leaders, when they change positions and have the ability to take their current assistants with them, do so? Because they know that what they have in that assistant is hard to come by; it can't easily be replaced. The assistant either has knowledge of the leader's habits, preferences, personality, communication style, work ethic or special expertise valuable to that leader. Perhaps their network has been invaluable to the leader's success.

Whatever the case, the current assistant is so worth keeping that it doesn't matter if the leader can hire someone else for less money – it's not worth taking the chance of losing what they have in that trusted individual.

When you move beyond focusing on the tasks themselves to the way those tasks are done: quickly, efficiently, proactively, with expertise and high quality, the performer of the tasks becomes much more important than the tasks themselves; in other words, *invaluable* – and in that case, you transform yourself from a commodity to a valuable asset, and *no one else* will do.

Helpful Analogies

Think of the way you shop for groceries. If you're value-minded, you don't mind buying generic brands for many common items because there's no discernable difference between the generic and the name brands.

However, there are probably certain items for which no generic can compare! For these items, you don't mind paying extra because they're worth it to you in terms of the quality of the taste, texture or versatility of the name brand item.

The same holds true for certain generic versus name brand drugs.

When I was younger, I suffered from migraine headaches. Thankfully, as I've gotten older, they have subsided to "normal" headaches! (Hey, if you have to have a headache, I'll take an "ordinary" one over a migraine any day.)

At one point, I found an incredible drug that relieved my migraines within one hour. However, my doctor felt (and the pharmacist agreed) that a generic drug would function the same as the name brand and have a lower co-pay on my insurance. So, I tried it.

Big mistake! Yes, the generic drug was cheaper, but it took four times as long and twice as many pills as the name brand drug to get any relief at all! If you've ever suffered with migraines, or know someone who has, you know that four minutes with a migraine feels like four hours, and four hours feels like four days… so any extra minute that it took to get relief was too much.

I gladly switched back to the name brand drug and paid the extra money, since it was well worth it in terms of the pain relief I experienced. (By the way, this is the only drug I've ever taken where there was any noticeable difference between the name brand and the generic.)

The game-changer: your vision for your career

In light of all this, I'd like you to set a new vision for your career: to be the best executive strategic partner you can be for your leader, their true right-hand person, and earn a seat at the executive table by becoming an asset to them and to the organization.

Think like the leader(s) you serve

If you want to advance your career and serve at a higher level, you must think – and speak – more like the leader(s) you serve. Think in terms of benefits and value; focus on outcomes rather than tasks. Then articulate that value in the language they use and in terms of the benefits *to them*.

You will never hear a leader talk about simply the tasks he/she does in their position. A leader talks about *how* they lead an organization to success… what their vision is for the organization, how their team will get there, their passion, the mission and values. In other words, all the things that comprise the added value they bring to the table by the way they lead the organization.

The tasks will follow based on what that leader wishes to accomplish. But it starts with the *why*, not with the *what* or *how*.

Of course, as assistants, much of your job has to be concerned with the "what" and the "how" – the logistical side… the side where you get things done.

But never start there. Start with the *why* and the benefits, and you will figure out what you need to do and, more importantly, *how* you need to do it. The *why* and the *how* are what create the experience for the leader and the organization.

The transition

When you focus on their experience with you, that opens the door to so many more opportunities to prove your value. This is where and how you make the following critical shift in your relationship:

Unknown ⟹ Believed ⟹ Believed In

Unknown: when you first begin at a job or company, you are an unknown quantity. They've read what you listed on your resume and cover letter, but how many people *lie* (or greatly exaggerate) their accomplishments on those documents? So, leaders are understandably wary of whether you can accomplish what you claim you can do.

Believed: After you've been with an organization or leader for a while, and have proved your capabilities, you move from being Unknown to being Believed. *"They can do all that – this is great!"*

Believed In: When you've proven, time after time, that you can not only do the job, but do it well, get things done, solve problems, even prevent other problems from happening, that's when you make a critical shift from being Believed to being Believed In. "I believe in your ability to do whatever needs to be done to help others, protect the organization, help it succeed…"

When you make this shift, you move from being Indispensable to being truly Invaluable to your leader and your organization.

Through the stories and examples contained in this book, you will see many principles and concepts in action and learn how to apply them to your specific position, so you can move into the Invaluable category in your organization.

Demonstrating your value

All of these revelations compelled me to create the following exercise and chart to enable assistants to re-consider the tasks they do in light of the value or benefit provided by the way they do them.

Exercise: Steps to maximize your value – what is your unique value?

1. List the top 10 tasks you do
2. List "extra" things you do to accomplish each task efficiently, cost-effectively, proactively, etc.
   a. Identify any specialized knowledge or tips you've acquired along the way (or brought with you to the position).
   b. Itemize the "unique" processes, procedures, or methods you use (or have created) to perform each task.
   c. Articulate the specific benefit(s) to your leader, co-workers, or organization (e.g., monetary, productivity, stress-relief, innovation/creativity/development).

Examples:

Task	How I do it	Benefit/value added
Research Process	• More in-depth analysis • Recognize and make pre-viously-unknown connections	• Leader doesn't have to think of everything up front; you've "got their back"! • Able to capitalize on important correlations others miss
Travel arrangements; calendar management	• Created Master Profile(s) for Leader(s): listed preferred airlines, routes, seating, times • Tech/system for co-ordinating schedules	• Less time wasted (no repeat instructions needed) • Travels worry- and stress-free • Meetings well organized, easy follow-up, no conflicts

Sandy Geroux, M.S.

Invaluable VS. Indispensable Worksheet

Task	How I do it	Benefit/value added

Chapter Two:

Hard-Hitting Tips From the Field

[2]

Hard-Hitting Tips From the Field

D uring my research for this topic, I interviewed many leaders, at all levels, to learn directly from them what they prized most in their assistants (current or former). The question I asked was this:

"If you think of the best assistants you've ever had (or known), what do you appreciate most about someone in that position?"

The answers to that question were widely varied, but 15 themes did emerge. This chapter will briefly outline those themes, which I've labelled "Tips," and they represent the traits and attitudes most often reported as "highly prized" by executives. Listed under each tip are several ideas (labeled **WOW** Ideas) and compelling stories to illustrate each one. Each idea is listed within the Tip it fits best, with all ideas sequentially numbered across Tips.

There are 36 ideas in total. I hope these will spark many more on your part as you read through each one and the accompanying stories that illustrate how to apply them in your position.

Tip #1

They consider themselves an extension of their leader

WOW *Idea #1*

Don't be slow or uninspired.

Our leaders are very concerned about the image being intentionally or inadvertently projected on their behalf. They know that the assistant is the public face of the office and that each visitor's experience at the assistant's desk reflects (and sometimes taints) their entire experience with everyone in that office.

One CEO told me this: *"If my assistant is smart, energetic, helpful, professional, then that's how people will see me and the entire team; if that person is slow or uninspired, that's what people will expect from me, too."*

So, be an exceptional administrative leader who is enthusiastic and energetic as you go about your duties. Of course, you're allowed a bad day or two, once in a while. We're all human. But don't let that be the norm. And don't frequently vacillate back and forth. Even if you are having a bad day, try to hide it as much as possible from the rest of your team.

Great leaders are not moody! No one wants to have to wonder who is going to greet them each day: Dr. Jekyll or Mr. Hyde. We've all worked with leaders whose team had to ask, *"What kind of a mood are they in today?"* before bringing anything to them. Don't be that person! It shuts down communication, demotivates the team and makes it nearly impossible to achieve your goals.

Tip #1 (continued)

They consider themselves an extension of their leader

WOW *Idea #2*

Be worthy of absolute trust regarding confidential information.

Practice keeping a neutral face when someone asks you about confidential information. Never divulge anything! People who are experts at reading body language can tell if you're nervous, avoiding an answer or even outright lying!

Lie detector equipment is effective for a reason! It can detect changes in heart rate, pulse, body temperature and a multitude of other symptoms when someone is uncomfortable with the topic at hand.

Practice keeping your face and voice neutral when someone asks you about this type of information. Your answer could be, *"I've heard that rumor. I can't confirm or deny that it's true."* Or you could just say, *"I can't discuss it."*

If they persist, don't speak! Just smile. The more you say, the more you give away. People are experts at stating what they know, hoping that the other person will assume they know more than they really do, and then "fill in" the gaps.

And don't lie! Those lies can (and will) catch up with you later. If you want to repeat one of the above phrases, do so. Then remove yourself from that situation as quickly as possible. Let them know you have to get on with your work… and then leave.

Tip #2

They have their leader's back

WOW *Idea #3*

Understand the people, culture and politics well enough to be an extra set of eyes and ears for your leader.

This doesn't mean to spy or "tattle" on others. It means being extremely observant, knowing your team well and building strong relationships because your leader can't be everywhere. And they can't know everything going on with everyone on their team.

One leader told me she asked her assistant to let her know when someone needed a little extra encouragement or celebration for something going on in their life. She also wanted to know when someone needed a "kick in the pants" to get them unstuck.

That was close!

While I was an executive assistant to one CEO, a dangerous situation arose, which he would have had no way of knowing if I hadn't found out and said something to him.

One of his direct reports was intentionally sabotaging his initiatives by telling his directors that they were not going to do what the CEO wanted, after promising the CEO that he would carry out his directives!

The only reason I found out was because the directors didn't feel comfortable going to the CEO directly, but they did feel comfortable talking to me. (Isn't that the way it often goes?) People often don't feel comfortable going to a higher-level leader, but because you've established great relationships with them, they do feel comfortable going to you, knowing you'll be able to find a way to address the situation.

I got permission from the directors to tell the CEO about their concerns; they assured me that if he came to them, they'd tell him the truth. But they just didn't feel comfortable going over their leader's head directly.

So, I told the CEO what was happening. I said, *"Don't take my word for it. You can ask the directors yourself."* So, he did. He discovered the truth about the sabotage and was able to diplomatically correct the situation.

I don't know what would have happened to the leader or the company if that high-level executive had been allowed to carry out his sabotage.

Tip #2 (continued)

They have their leader's back

WOW *Idea #4*

Buy greeting cards for every occasion at the beginning of every month. Have your leader sign them all up front; give them out (from your leader) on the proper day.

As I mentioned before (and you well know), your leader can't be everywhere and know everything, especially if the team is large or spread out. But you often can.

Make it a point to learn (and log) everyone's birthdays, anniversaries, work anniversaries and other important dates. Many companies have databases that track these items. If you don't have a central database, create one for your team and set calendar appointments to deliver or mail the cards at the appropriate times.

The beauty of this is that the card doesn't have to be delivered by the leader; the important part is that for at least one minute the leader was thinking of that person and writing a personal greeting to them. The delivery method is not an issue. What matters is that it's important for your leaders to be connected with their people.

Seasons Personal Greetings!

I worked for one CEO who had 2,000 employees spread out in offices across the U.S. Every December holiday season, he hand-wrote a personal note in a greeting card to each one. The surprising thing was that these cards did not contain a standard, *"Happy Holidays!"* message. Every message was personal because the CEO made it a point to get to know every one of his employees. If an employee was too new at holiday time, he wrote a note saying that he was looking forward to getting to know that employee better… and then he did it!

For months prior to the holidays, he took stacks of cards with him everywhere he went. If he was sitting on a plane, watching TV at night, or just had a few minutes while waiting for a meeting to start, he was signing cards. It was that important that he let his people know he cared about them.

Because of this, they loved him! In fact, he was one of the best leaders for whom I've ever worked.

Your leaders don't have to go to this extreme, but with your help they can find a way to honor and emotionally reward everyone on the team.

Happy Holidays

Tip #3

They are extremely detail-oriented

WOW *Idea #5*

Never assume! (you know what they say…)

One thing to watch for is to make the subtle connections that most people miss by assuming everything is going to work as planned.

Has anything ever worked as planned, especially the first time you try it? For me, it usually hasn't! I've developed a habit of creating backup plans for my backup plans, and also double-checking that everything I expected to happen did.

Who knew?

For example, my husband and I worked together as programmer and Business Systems Consultant/Systems Analyst on a large project to create a technology system for a university. On a weekend when we planned to install an upgrade to the system, everyone was notified well in advance that the system would be down for that weekend while we worked on it.

However, when we tried to work on the system on that weekend, we couldn't get into it! We tried every contact we had, none of whom could reach anyone who knew why we were unable to access the system. On Monday morning, the university had to issue a statement notifying everyone that the planned upgrade did not happen on the weekend, and that the system would be down on the following weekend for the upgrade.

Kind of sounds like it was our fault, doesn't it? (I hate it when that happens!)

Well, we discovered on Monday morning, there had been a power failure at the university on the previous Friday evening. All systems are set to automatically come up after such an event... all systems, that is, except the network that contained the database we needed to access; *that* network needed to be manually restarted after any power outage.

Apparently, only <u>one</u> person at the university knew this! But they had failed to share that information with anyone else, so when the power outage happened after hours, they couldn't be reached and no one else knew how to fix the issue.

Everyone ended up with egg on their face after that event. But it did point out a gap in their contingency systems that they were able to close. The assumptions that allowed this issue to happen were numerous:

- Power outages would only happen while the one person who knew how to restore all systems was on site (or at least accessible);
- Everything would work correctly after a power outage, so no tests needed to be conducted that simulated a power outage;
- More than one person knew how to deal with this type of situation OR that person would have shared this information with others;
- Backup personnel are not needed for critical systems;
- I could go on and on...

The upshot is never assume! Ask questions. Test scenarios. Cross-train.

Some people believe "Knowledge is Power," so they hoard it to increase their power. But knowledge is only power if you share it. Sharing your knowledge doesn't make you *less* valuable. It makes you *in*valuable because you had the foresight and commitment to excellence to prevent a problem from happening.

Tip #3 (continued)

They are extremely detail-oriented

WOW *Idea #6*

Make a list of everyone who needs to know what information, so you can quickly disseminate it when needed. Keep all contact information up to date.

This will definitely help with the previous example, especially if you insist on capturing the off-site contact information (for emergency use only) of anyone in a critical role that could shut the organization down if they can't be reached.

In addition to helping prevent disasters, keeping lists of everyone on the Administrative Team and their specialized knowledge and talents is also helpful. Think back to the last time you struggled with something that took you an hour to figure out because it was not your forte. Now imagine how productive you could have been if you'd had the name and number of someone very familiar with that system or tool who could have helped you get over that hurdle in five minutes!

Thank you for your help!

I've had many of my speaking colleagues call me with technical questions on MS Word, PowerPoint, Excel and more because I used to be a hands-on tech trainer and know these systems inside and out. They often call and ask me a question, which I answer by picturing in my head the appropriate screens and menus and walking them through the steps they need to take.

Wouldn't it be great if we all had resources like that?

Well, we do! The problem is that those talents are often hidden because no one has taken the time to ask what everyone is great at and whether they'd be willing and able to help with it, then put a database together that is shared by all.

You can strengthen the power and impact of your entire Administrative Team by putting a database like this together and enabling everyone on the team to quickly and easily help each other.

Tip #3 (continued)

They are extremely detail-oriented

WOW *Idea #7*

Take responsibility for updating lists when people come and go. Don't let these lists become outdated.

This is related to Idea #6 because it's no use to have a list if it isn't kept up to date. Also, check with other departments to see if they are keeping duplicate (or partially duplicate) lists of their own. Never assume a list is being updated simply because it exists.

Talk about extra work!

Many times, I have gone into organizations and we've all discovered (together) that several departments are keeping lists with many of the same names on them.

Not only does this duplicate the same effort in multiple departments, but often one list is updated while another isn't, simply because no one knew that another list existed!

Create a Master List that can be updated by one person and accessed by everyone who needs that information. Or create shared lists that are updated by many but accessible to all. If certain names should not be accessed by everyone, there are ways to keep that information from being accessed by either assigning privileges regarding who can access what information.

But do yourself a favor and keep master lists that have people assigned to keeping them current and let everyone access the appropriate information.

I thought he was slacking off lately!

In another case, the team discovered that someone's name was still on a list three years after he had passed away!

Much of this type of challenge comes from the fact that there is no master list, and even if there is one, no one is assigned to update it!

I'm reminded of the story of four people: Anyone, everyone, someone and no one.

There was a job to be done. Anyone could have done it. Everyone thought someone would do it. But no one did it… so the job didn't get done.

Don't let these four people sabotage your organization's success!

Tip #4

They are proactive

WOW *Idea #8*

When you see something that needs to be done (and you are able to do it), just do it.

You don't always have to ask permission to do things that need to be done. Of course, you must be careful not to overstep your bounds; you also don't want to end up doing everyone else's work and reinforcing the fact that if they leave it long enough, you'll just take care of it.

But if there is something simple that you can easily take care of, and you can pitch in and help, don't wait for someone else to do it.

If there's a project you'd like to tackle, or your leader is overloaded, ask permission to take care of that project for her.

You deserve an award!

For example, one leader told me that she was responsible for coordinating an employee rewards banquet, which was an incredible amount of work added to her already-full plate. So, her assistant asked if she could take over the project. She and her project team arranged for the banquet room, ordered the menu, created and sent invitations, managed the guest list, arranged for decorations, and even made certificates for the employees receiving awards! She kept her leader informed along the way, so there were no surprises. But this high-functioning partnership between the leader and her assistant allowed the job to get done beautifully without the leader having to take everything on herself.

What can you do to alleviate the burden on your leader? If you're interested in a project, let your hidden talents and interests be known, so you can be considered for not only that project, but future similar projects.

Your leaders will never think of you for anything other than what they see you already doing if you don't speak up and let them know you're interested.

One way to get permission to try new things is to reduce the risk for your leader. If they are very risk-averse, it may be difficult to get them to say yes or to let go of tasks that they have always performed themselves.

If you've ever thought to yourself, *"If you want something done right, you've got to do it yourself,"* you know what they must be feeling. Yes, they fall into the same traps you do because they're human, too! So, they often believe that they must be the one to perform certain tasks they're used to doing themselves.

Now, why didn't I think of that?

My own husband fell into this trap! One of his assistants was a very competent, very personable young woman named Linda, and we both liked her very much. He complained to me one time, many years after leaving that job, that in that position he had to create a weekly status report for his boss that took a ton of his time. He compiled the report from status reports collected by Linda from his direct reports and including the pertinent information in his own report.

I asked him why he didn't have Linda create the report for him, and he immediately said, *"Oh, no! She can't do that! I have to do it!"*

I looked him in the eye and asked, *"Why couldn't she do it? Is she not smart enough?"*

He answered, *"No, it's not that! She just wouldn't know what to include."*

So, I made a suggestion: What if he prepared his report as usual and Linda prepared one of her own from the same data. They could compare the reports, with him coaching her on any items she'd overlooked. After just a few weeks of doing the reports in tandem, I was sure that Linda was smart enough to grasp the topics and updates important enough to be included in his report, and she could take it off his plate.

If he was going to have to do the reports anyway, why not try this very low-risk solution and see how it worked out?

I asked, *"Would that have been acceptable?"*

He looked at me and said, *"Now why didn't I ever think of that? Yes, that would have been great!"*

Sometimes our leaders are just too busy with their own work to even think of alternate solutions; other times they are just a bit nervous about not getting the job done well or on time, or at all!

But doing a task in tandem with them could be a great low-risk way to get someone to say yes to allowing you to try new things!

Tip #4 (continued)

They are proactive

WOW *Idea #9*

When you see something that no longer needs to be done, test its necessity and, if appropriate, get permission to stop doing it.

Too often, tasks are repeated at companies long after they are no longer necessary, simply because no one questions their necessity – or possibly no one has time to question it and change things.

However, the following story illustrates how productive and cost-efficient we can become if we start eliminating unnecessary tasks that are being done just because *"that's the way it's always been done."*

I'm so glad you asked!

One leader told me that their organization had been creating three large reports every week. Her assistant approached her one day and told her she didn't think anyone was reading them and requested permission to stop sending them out. She would continue to create them, just in case, but not distribute them. She wanted to see if anyone missed them.

The leader gave permission for the test and in the first week, two of the reports never even received an inquiry. The third did, so she sent that one out. She repeated the experiment for the next four weeks and no one ever missed two out of the three reports. So, they stopped producing them.

The labor cost savings involved in not forcing all the people on the team to go through the motions of getting the information for those two reports was calculated to save the company $50,000 per year in labor costs!

Tip #4 (continued)

They are proactive

WOW *Idea #10*

Think of what would "never happen" and prepare for it.

Have backup flights, hotels, cars, transportation on any business trip.
Provide paper copies of critical travel documents, just in case.

"May I see your boarding pass, please?"

One leader told me that his assistant had provided him with a paper copy of his boarding pass on a flight scheduled to depart just after a major airline's reservation system was hacked. No one with electronic tickets were allowed on the plane because the system couldn't scan the documents to verify that they were authentic. The only passengers allowed to get on any flight until the problem was resolved were those with paper boarding passes.

Focus on their experience — not just the task at hand.

I know we're trying to save trees by not printing everything out. But this once again assumes that all will go perfectly with technology — and that isn't always practical. Save trees whenever you can, but if an item is critical for a job to be completed, and it relies solely on technology working perfectly in order to succeed, I wouldn't sacrifice the safety of my leader or the success of a critical project by not printing those few crucial items. I'll save the trees elsewhere!

Even if it isn't "life or death," here's an important concept I'd like to stress: Focus on their experience – not just the task at hand.

What an experience!

One leader told me that she had an assistant she would never forget, even though she hadn't worked with her for 23 years!

She and her entire team had a meeting in Denver, Colorado. The assistant made all the travel arrangements for them. It was to be a flight to Denver for a meeting that would last several hours, then a flight home.

On the day of the trip, the team got to Denver, but a huge snowstorm moved in while they were in the meeting. The meeting room had no windows, so the meeting participants couldn't see the storm raging outside.

Most of us know that Denver experiences a LOT of snow, so hearing that a snowstorm was coming wouldn't have been cause for alarm. Therefore, many assistants would likely have assumed that the city and the airport would have been able to handle a simple snowstorm… and just assumed everything would be OK. The arrangements were already set; now on to the next task!

But this forward-thinking assistant had kept her eye on the weather (years before there were smartphones and weather apps!) and when she saw that this was no simple snowstorm, she took it upon herself to re-book her team on an earlier flight, then call the meeting location and tell her leader to get everyone to the airport for an earlier flight home, which they did.

It turned out that they were on the very last flight to leave Denver for 48 hours! The rest of the meeting participants spent a very uncomfortable two days at the Denver airport because all hotels were filled by the time they realized what was happening. Their assistants hadn't thought to keep an eye on the weather; they assumed it would be just another day in snowy Denver. As a result, everyone was unpleasantly surprised when it turned out to be otherwise.

Let's break down what happened: yes, every assistant accomplished their TASK of getting their teams to the meeting and getting them home... eventually. But most of them accomplished that task UGLY! The experience for the travelers was horrendous, uncomfortable and unproductive for days! And there was a chance it could have been avoided if their assistants had not "assumed." Only one provided the kind of experience any traveler would desire.

Think proactively of every situation in which an unknown quantity could derail your leader's experience and the experience of their teams. Are they traveling to areas of extreme weather? Political unrest? Other factors?

The more often you can think ahead and plan for almost any contingency, the less often you and your leader will be unpleasantly surprised by the experience that follows.

Tip #5

They have the "Radar O'Reilly Factor"

WOW *Idea #11*

Provide what your leader needs, even before they know they need it.

Those of us who are of (ahem) a certain age remember the TV show, "M*A*S*H," a hysterical comedy about a Mobile Army Surgical Hospital in Korea during the Korean War. Younger folks might also know of this show because it has been in reruns forever!

In the show, one of the main characters is Corporal Walter O'Reilly, who seems to know what's going to happen before everyone else, such as when helicopters (or choppers, as they called them) are arriving with wounded soldiers, and what his Colonel needs before he even asks for it! It's so obvious that he has a "gift" that this is where he got his nickname *"Radar."*

However, Radar really didn't have ESP or any other magical powers that we mere mortals don't possess. What was really happening was that Radar had exceptional hearing, combined with the fact that he was so "tuned in" to what his people needed and to his surroundings that it looked like he knew what was going to happen before it did.

In fact, we can all be Radar O'Reillys if we pay as close attention as he did.

First, he was so committed to excellence that he was always cognizant of his surroundings, always listening for the blades of the choppers so he could warn the entire camp to be prepared as soon as possible to treat the critically wounded soldiers who would be relying on them to try to save their lives. Because of that focus, he "heard" – more likely noticed and recognized – the sound of the chopper blades a hair earlier than the others.

Think of a situation where you are very familiar with the somewhat unusual sounds, sights or smells associated with it. You can recognize those sensory items a little sooner than others who are either not familiar with them or not focused on listening or watching for them, can't you? That's because you've become attuned to them. It's the same principle with Radar.

Second, Radar was so competent in his job that he knew what was needed in any given situation. This was no small task, given the number of forms the Army had and the crazy letters by which they referred to them!

Because his hearing was great and he was always paying attention to what was going on around him, he often heard his Colonel's conversations, since his desk was right outside the Colonel's office... both located in a tent without real walls or soundproofing.

So, when he would hear the Colonel talk about needing a piece of medical equipment, for example, Radar was already walking into the office with the needed paperwork when the Colonel started to yell out, *"Radar, can you bring me a 437 - stroke - R2 Form?"*

In the TV show, it became a running joke and the Colonel once said to Radar, *"Would you please wait for me to ask for the form before you bring it to me?!"*

But in real life, wouldn't it be great if you could anticipate many of your leader's needs and provide what they needed quickly and efficiently, seemingly before they even know they need it?

Oh, you're an angel!

Several leaders shared stories with me of their assistants being so attuned to their moods, needs and even the craziness of their days that they would often get little surprises when they got to their office.

One would get their leader a nice hot Starbucks, or tea or a piece of chocolate that would be waiting on their desk when they returned from a tough meeting. Personally, I'll take a Drake's Devil Dog or Yodel any day!

One executive assistant told me that they gave their leader a small thank you card for being so supportive and understanding toward them. The leader was so touched and appreciative of the note that he brought it home to show his wife.

As I've mentioned before, leaders are people, too. And as much as we appreciate a little compassion or an "Attaboy!" or "Attagirl!" once in a while, our leaders don't often receive that luxury. You can be that small bright spot in a tough day for them.

Tip #5 (Continued)

They have the "Radar O'Reilly Factor"

WOW *Idea #12*

When you (over)hear someone say they need something done, do it before they ask.

People are usually pleasantly surprised to find that something they need done is already taken care of without their having to ask (sometimes multiple times), drag someone away from another task, handhold and teach someone else or do it themselves.

Any time you can alleviate their burden by taking care of something before they ask, it only helps reinforce the *invaluable* nature of your presence as that person's executive partner.

Already taken care of!

One leader told me that there would be multiple times throughout the day when he would ask his assistant to do something and hear, *"Already done!"*

A prime example of this was when he was chosen to lead a new Board of Directors and needed to set up monthly board meetings. Knowing how busy everyone was, his assistant took it upon herself to contact everyone with potential meeting times for the next 12 months, coordinate their availability and get the meetings scheduled onto everyone's calendars before they filled up! He was very pleasantly surprised when she told him she'd done this!

Tip #6

They are incredibly organized

WOW *Idea #13*

Create systems to organize your space and track projects… and share them with your leader.

Earlier in this book, I mentioned that when you are indispensable, you can never take time off or be out of communication, because everything would fall apart. This is not a desirable situation.

While certain pieces of knowledge cannot easily be transferred to another person, others can be, which eases your burden by providing simple solutions that others can follow. That includes your leader. Teaching your leader at least some of your systems makes them much more productive if you are ever absent because they won't be clueless to handle certain tasks or find needed information.

Can you teach that to my assistant?

In one of my administrative positions, I had to reorganize my executive's files and create a filing system that made sense. I wanted to create a system that I could easily remember and, more importantly, teach him in case I was absent some day and he needed something from the files.

So, I created a color-coded system. Each file cabinet drawer represented a different category and the contents of the files within were easily recognizable by the color of their tabs. In the front of each drawer, I created a list of the files in that drawer; and in the front of the top drawer was a Master List of drawer categories.

Don't worry about the old "Knowledge is Power" factor.

It was easy to create and teach to my executive. If I happened to be away from my desk at any given time when he needed something from the file, he didn't have to either wait, search frantically for me or the files, or make anyone else wait for an answer that was easily obtainable in the files. He loved it!

One day, when another executive walked by my desk and saw my executive quickly getting something from the file cabinet, he asked how he was able to find what he needed so quickly. My executive told him of my system and when I returned to my desk, he asked if I would teach that system to his assistant because he could never find anything in the files when she wasn't around!

The same principles can be applied to electronic files now, which I use for email and file storage on my hard drives. They can still be organized, color-coded and placed in a common repository that you can both understand. There are even indexed, search-enabled services you can use.

Again, don't worry about the old "Knowledge is Power" factor. Your power is not in the knowledge you hoard; it's in the leadership you show by enabling others around you to succeed on their own.

After all, it's not like the comedy TV show "Everybody Loves Raymond," where Ray's mother, Marie, tells her husband Frank that he can cook his own dinner because she's sick of waiting on him without receiving any appreciation.

Frank's retort? *"If I could do that, you'd be out on the curb!"*

Tip #7

They know and understand the needs of their leader

WOW *Idea #14*

Be patient (and forgiving) if your leader snaps at you out of frustration or impatience.

If this is not their usual way of communicating with others, understand that sometimes they get frustrated and impatient at times and may take it out on the one(s) closest to them (much like a marriage). The same is true if you don't receive praise and recognition from your leader as often as you wish... or ever!

Don't take it personally. It may not be in their nature to praise others often, although great leaders recognize this in themselves and try to overcome the negative tendencies to ignore the work of their team members.

Take the fact that you still have a job and they trust you with many things as a sign of their praise and approval. And, if possible, help them understand (without judgment) that it would inspire the team a great deal more, including yourself, if they occasionally handed out a kind comment or word of encouragement and validation for their efforts.

Tip #7 (Continued)

They know and understand the needs of their leader

WOW *Idea #15*

Be a relationship-builder. Avoid getting caught up in petty grievances. If possible, keep them from your leader's desk, as well.

One of the biggest challenges any leader must contend with is getting involved in petty office grievances. The problems of "who did what to whom" need to be resolved, as much as possible, *before they hit the leader's office.*

Sometimes you can assist with these efforts; other times you can't. As often as possible, avoid creating, exacerbating or indulging them yourself.

Be very careful not to tacitly agree with someone engaging in office gossip, bullying or other harmful forms of communication. Not only do you want to avoid the appearance that you agree with the communication, but it could also be incorrectly inferred that your leader holds the same opinion. This goes back to one of the very first tips in this book: you are an extension of the leader and your actions, behaviors, opinions and other communications reflect on them.

If someone directs these types of comments to you, and you say nothing, it could be taken to mean that you agree with them. It's best to firmly and diplomatically let them know that you do not agree with their opinion and do not wish to discuss the topic further.

For example, if someone comes to you and complains about someone, you can simply reply, *"That hasn't been my experience with that person, and I don't want to comment on that."* If they persist, you can again tell them that you really don't want to discuss it, then move on to other topics.

Be sure to try to discuss something else with them, so they don't leave with hurt feelings and a "sour" taste in their mouth from their interaction with you. Your intention is not to cause hurt feelings, but to stop the gossip-related conversation. **If you don't discuss something else with them to end the conversation on a positive note and let them know that you don't harbor any ill feelings toward them, they may go away with the wrong impression.** This could cause them to be uncomfortable talking to you again, which can escalate the hard feelings, even if they exist only in their own mind.

You probably realize that an argument or a change in a relationship can often take on a life of its own. Try not to let a negative tone stand at the end of any discussion, so you can lessen the possibility of this happening in your relationships.

This situation is exacerbated by the fact that many of us are working virtually, a topic which I will be covering in my blog at www.wowplace.com

Tip #7 (Continued)

They know and understand the needs of their leader

WOW *Idea #16*

Use one of the techniques of Indirect Influence the next time you need to ask for something.

Your leader often relies on you to accomplish goals beyond the typical scope of your position, especially when they don't have time to do it themselves.

When you don't have the authority or rank to go with the requests you are often required to make, one of the 7 Techniques of Indirect Influence can help.

They are listed below and are reprinted with permission. (Original article available from ManageTrainLearn at www.ManageTrainLearn.com.)

1. "What if…?"

    A "what if…" question is a hypothetical way of gently suggesting a solution to a problem.

    "What if we computerized…?"

2. 2nd Person Quote

    By talking about your solution as if it were happening to someone else, your boss will relate the story to his or her own situation.

    "I know Accounts has the same problem and used consultants."

3. Softeners

    Softeners put proposals in ways that give the boss room to think…
    "Do you think it might help if…" "I wonder whether…?" "Maybe…"

4. Visual Metaphor

    The visual metaphor helps the boss to see things in a different way.
    "This problem's like untangling spaghetti…"

5. Repeated "yes"

    Several repeated "yeses" from the boss puts them in a favorable frame
    of mind for your solution.
    "We do need more business, don't we?"
    "We need more revenue, wouldn't you agree?"
    "A computer would be more efficient, wouldn't it?"

6. Presupposition

    A presupposition gets your boss to mentally accept your solution.
    "What software would we need for a computer like this?"

7. Modest influence

    Modest influence is a way to put forward a view to your boss without
    arguing it with certainty.
    "If I'm not mistaken…" or *"I'm fairly sure it will work."*

Tip #8

They have a sense of urgency

WOW *Idea #17*

Let your leader know you're taking a situation seriously, even if you're not acting on it immediately.

One of the worst things you can do is cause your leader to believe that you don't have a sense of urgency about one of their requests. That's not to say that you have to jump every time they bring something to you. But it does mean that you have to respond in a way that reassures them that you'll take care of it in the appropriate timeframe.

Just because someone brings a task to you doesn't mean it's a true emergency, whether they think so or not. If you're in the middle of something else, ask a few clarifying questions. Make it clear that you're not questioning the *need* to do the task, just the *timing* of it.

You could say, *"Is this something that needs to be done immediately, or can I take care of it in two hours, when I'm finished with the current high-priority task I'm working on now?"*

No one minds clarifying questions! What they do mind is either the attitude that you're not taking it seriously, not going to do it or are annoyed by the request.

Even worse is when you ignore the person or the task. *You* may know that you will get to it in an hour, but how would *they* know unless you tell them? Never make them wonder when (or if) it will actually get done.

One of the biggest problems with this type of scenario is that people don' clarify the timing, and plan to "get to it" in a little while without telling the othe person of their plans; or they silently fume while they do a task that wasn't urgent

The other problem is that we often fail to take human nature into account Why is that person bringing this task to you now, when it isn't even urgent? The answer often is, *"So they don't forget about it!"* They figure if they dump the task on your desk, it's now your problem and not theirs! They've done their part (before they forget to do it); now it's up to you to finish it.

And we let them! By doing so, we're rewarding them for doing it. In othe words, we're rewarding the wrong behavior!

The majority of these tasks and their related unnecessary stress could be lessened or eliminated if we just start managing expectations and rewarding the right behavior.

For example, when someone puts something on your desk, despite the fac that you look incredibly busy, you can accept the task, clarify the timing and le them know when it will be done.

But then go one step further and ask them to, for example, please put those types of requests in an email to you, especially if they require lots of instructions You don't have to make them go back and do it that time but suggest it for the future. This allows them to accomplish their goal of getting that task off their list before they forget, it (hopefully) becomes much clearer when they put it in writing and you get the ability to schedule it into your day or week, as necessary.

This may not work every time or with every leader. But try it anyway. After all, what have you got to lose? If they refuse to do it, you're no worse off than before. And if they agree, you'll both come out ahead!

Tip #8 (Continued)

They have a sense of urgency

WOW *Idea #18*

Calm down someone who is panicking by asking them to breathe, and then identify the problem and what you can do at that moment to help them.

When someone is panicking, stay calm. You can be their "safe harbor" in the storm if you keep your wits about you.

Monitored breathing is one of the best ways to calm down. It forces your body to take a short rest and allows more oxygen to reach your brain, which helps you think better.

Once they calm down enough to tell you what is going on, have them home in on the ONE task that you can do immediately to help them the most. Often when you complete that first task, it offers a little more breathing room to get the rest of the team together if necessary, accomplish the next task or make a plan.

So, don't join them in hitting the Panic Button… help them calm down those warning lights and sirens and get to a place of emotional safety. They will appreciate your cool head and ability to act effectively under duress.

Tip #9

They have a positive attitude

WOW *Idea #19*

Start each day with gratitude.

Take two minutes before you get out of bed each morning to focus on something for which you are grateful, something positive in your life.

This is especially important when things all around you are going wrong and it's natural to immediately think of all the negative things surrounding those events. You focus on them and allow them to swallow you up, which taints everything else in your life.

You can't have a positive attitude without consciously focusing on the good things all around you every day. For some people this comes more naturally than for others. But even the most positive person can succumb if they allow the negative things in life to consume them and fill their thoughts.

Many of us do this at family times, holidays and other special times. Now make it a habit to do it as a matter of course every day. You'll be surprised at the difference it makes! Remember, you will be no good to your leader or your organization if you are negative.

Tip #9 (Continued)

They have a positive attitude

WOW *Idea #20*

Set (and demonstrate) a positive mood from the top.

A positive attitude is different than a positive mood. Most people who have a positive attitude experience a foul mood occasionally. They wouldn't be human otherwise. But the importance of this distinction when serving in any leadership position (business or family) is realizing the mood you set from the top. Whatever your mood is will often be reflected in your team. This is illustrated in a concept called **Systems Theory**.

Systems Theory maintains that everyone is part of the system as a whole, and the parts cannot and do not operate independently of each other. Anyone who thinks, *"It's not their problem – it's mine,"* is sadly mistaken. Your frame of mind and behavior (as well as your leader's) affect everyone with whom you interact.

When no one can tell what kind of mood the leader (and all of the leader's executive partners) will be in each day, it turns the entire department into babbling fools who are unable to accomplish tasks because they are too afraid to ask for guidance, admit mistakes or even talk to someone for fear of retribution.

So, ensure that you and your leader(s) set the right tone from the top.

Tip #10

They can slide in to fill the gaps

WOW *Idea #21*

Don't shut down your leader's office just because your leader is out.

Does your office shut down when the leader is not there? How frustrating is it when you experience this with other departments?

It's important that you are knowledgeable, flexible, willing and versatile enough to help out wherever needed. In fact, the words one leader used to describe what he expected from his assistants were these: *"They can serve as an intermediary for me."*

This means that if a message needs to be given, you can sometimes give it to the recipient in your leader's absence; you can handle basic questions that arise or defuse any challenges without getting upset or defensive (on your behalf or your leader's) or making the situation worse.

Of course, this applies only to appropriate situations; some situations need to wait for the leader's return – or at least for the leader to step in from out of town. But if you truly are your leader's "right-hand person," there are many situations where you can fill the gap left by their temporary absence.

Tip #10 (Continued)

They can slide in to fill the gaps

WOW *Idea #22*

Volunteer to help someone else if you have time in your schedule.

How often have you needed help that just wasn't available? Wouldn't you have appreciated it if someone would have stepped up and offered to help you, even with a small, short task? That's one less thing for you to do!

So, especially at times when your leader is not present, or you have a lull between projects, build relationships by asking what you can do for someone else. The best networkers are those who understand that helping is a two-way street.

Build better relationships by being the first to ask how you can help. You never know when the street might go the other way and you'll be the one asking for help. Not only will you make your leader look good for hiring such a caring and compassionate assistant (and being compassionate enough *themselves* to allow their assistant to help others), but executives at your leader's level will appreciate the help you offer to their teams, which helps you expand your network and your influence further throughout the organization.

Tip #10 (Continued)

They can slide in to fill the gaps

WOW *Idea #23*

Do the "impossible" – at least, give it everything you've got.

As an assistant, you're often asked to do the "impossible." And for a surprising percentage of the time, you do it! When your leader asks, *"Can you take care of this?"* your automatic answer is, *"Yes!"* Of course, your next thought is, *"Oh my goodness, how am I going to do this?"!*

You may have to call in favors, tap your network, build relationships or bridges, but you pull out all the stops to get it done.

That was amazing!

When one leader was planning an event for VIPs at a children's hospital, he turned to his soon-to-be Personal Assistant (you read that right, she didn't even formally work for him yet!) and asked her to make it happen with only two days notice! Within a week of being hired, he also asked her to arrange another event for over 200 people taking place the following week.

She accomplished both events in grand style, arranging for a harbor cruise for close VIPs, friends and family, car services and a cocktail reception (donated at no charge) at Ronald McDonald House.

Prior to this role, she was even able to arrange a backstage meet-and-greet with a celebrity musician for her VIP-level attendees.

Both the donated cocktail reception and the meet-and-greet were made possible only through connections she had previously made at conferences for administrative professionals. She was also able to delegate various duties to several high-level EAs in her local area who volunteered to help her on site on the night of the second event (during their free time!), which she would have been unable to handle alone.

"Without my connections and their generosity in offering their expertise and their time," she says, *"there's no way I would have been able to pull off either one of those events."*

Her latest accomplishment occurred when she was asked to contact a prominent world figure who was difficult to reach; of course, she came through. How did she do it? You guessed it: by tapping into the connections *of* connections she had made at an event for executive assistants.

This brings up the topic of **networking:** Over the years, networking at training events focused on assistants has helped this assistant (and many others) grow her knowledge and skills much more quickly than if she'd tried to do it on her own. And when asked to do the "impossible," networking is often how things get done.

There are many opportunities to network, but you don't have to wait for special events. Just pick up the phone and call someone – in your company or outside of it! The worst they can do is say "no." But if they say "yes," you've started a relationship and can find a way to reciprocate.

You never know when you will need someone's help or who they know. And you can't wait until you need someone before you start building relationships. Start building them early on and put yourself in the best position to help and be helped when needed.

Tip #11

They have a service orientation

WOW *Idea #24*

Learn their preferences for everything: travel, restaurants, snacks, coffee, communication vehicles, leadership styles – and more!

When you pay attention to these things, you can anticipate their needs and provide things without being asked – again, the "Radar O'Reilly" factor!

But more than that, it shows that you have a genuine interest in the other person, and that makes for an obvious service orientation.

We can all claim to be service-oriented *("That's our job!")* but proving it in all the big and small ways that create **WOW** experiences for others is another thing. If someone has to constantly repeat their preferences, answer the same questions over and over or just do it themselves because it's easier than explaining the whole thing one more time, that's an OW experience.

But these small nuances are where the experience changes. They will be pleasantly surprised when you remember or notice something they thought you didn't notice… or didn't have time to notice. It can show up in the previous examples of leaving snacks on their desk or in giving gifts to them.

Or it can show up in your knowledge of the way they like to communicate, preferred times for visitors and meetings, leadership styles, and more. Surprise and delight them with your care, concern and knowledge of them at every turn!

Tip #11 (Continued)

They have a service orientation

WOW *Idea #25*

Don't get insulted by the occasional request for a personal favor, such as getting coffee or picking something up at the store.

We all need a little extra help once in a while. So, if your leader asks you to occasionally do what is now often considered to be a "menial" task, don't get insulted by those requests! Take it from the source. If your leader is usually kind and considerate and would do those things for you (if possible), why not reciprocate? They probably aren't trying to insult you or put you in the "1950s secretarial box."

I've had several leaders who have offered to get me coffee while they're on their way to get a cup themselves. I'd have done that for them in a heartbeat!

Sandy Geroux, M.S.

Tip #12

They have a sense of humor

WOW *Idea #26*
Brighten your leader's day with periodic surprise laughs or chuckles.

I could write an entire book on this topic alone! There are so many ways for us to use humor in the workplace – and everywhere in life! Where do I begin?

Let me start with a few stories that will give you ideas on how to use great humor in the workplace to accomplish many things: lessen stress, break tension, teach a lesson and even get things done!

You're kidding me!

One leader told me that she loves the show, "Miami Vice." The main character, Sonny Crockett, was played by an actor named Don Johnson.

One day, a different man named Don Johnson called her office and her assistant decided to have some fun with her. Instead of just putting his name on her e-mail message, she added the Miami Vice logo and wrote in the subject line *"Don Johnson called!"*

In the body of the email, she started with, *"Just kidding!"* and proceeded to explain that it was a different Don Johnson.

It was just a small, little bit of humor, but dished out sporadically throughout a day or week, it can make your environment more fun.

56

Tip #12 (Continued)

They have a sense of humor

WOW *Idea #27*

Keep a humor file.

When things get too tense, a humor file is a great tool you can use to take a one-minute break and have a good laugh.

Milton Berle, the old-time comedian, once said, *"Laughter is an instant vacation."* It's so true! Don't you feel like you've had a little vacation when you've shared a good laugh with someone? I do!

So, keep a few items on hand that make you laugh, or even just smile. You can print them or keep them on your phone or laptop. Just keep them within reach so you can pull them out, give yourself a short break from the tension and then get back to what you were doing.

I keep jokes, cartoons and other fun items in mine. They make me smile *every time* I look at them!

Tip #12 (Continued)

They have a sense of humor

WOW *Idea #28*

Use your sense of humor to connect with someone, alleviate a tense situation or get something done (when asking, pleading and "lecturing" don't work).

You're hired!

I was in the market for an Executive Assistant/Office Manager at one time and placed an ad in the paper. I received 52 responses to one ad, and set up 12 appointments.

My very first appointment was with a woman named Wendy, who was very qualified for the position. At the end of the interview, I told her I really enjoyed our interview but couldn't offer the position to anyone yet, as I still had 11 other appointments scheduled.

She said she understood, but then turned to me with this sly smile and said, *"Unless, of course, you'd like me to call the other candidates and let them know the position has been filled!"*

Go, Wendy! She got me and my sense of humor in a heartbeat! I didn't want to work with an old "stick-in-the-mud!" She let me know right there that it would be fun working with her.

I didn't offer the position to her at that time (although I appreciated her humor), but guess who every candidate from that point on was compared with? Right, Wendy! And guess who got the job? Right again, Wendy!

Letting someone see your sense of humor can connect very well with someone who has a similar attitude. And that can make for a beautiful partnership.

Stop stealing our pencils!

My sister told me of a situation at the university where she worked, where someone was continually stealing pencils from the ESL (English as a Second Language) department. Department leaders had tried everything to get people to stop: sending emails, asking if anyone saw the "thief" and basically pleading for it to stop... to no avail.

One day, a creative member of the department took to PhotoShop to create an image that was sent to everyone in the university in an email. The image was of a cardboard milk carton, similar to the ones where the photos of Missing Children are placed. But the photos on this one were of a bunch of pencils, with the word MISSING at the top.

There were two photos: one of a group of beautiful, freshly-sharpened pencils, labeled *"How the pencils looked on the day they went missing."* The second photo was of short, stubby, chewed-up pencils. This photo was labeled *"FBI-age-enhanced photo of how the pencils might look today."*

The photos came from the "National Center for Missing & Exploited Office Supplies" and the phone number to call was 1-800-YOU-CANT-BE-SERIOUS!

Hysterical! And it worked... the pencils stopped disappearing!

So, get creative and you can use your sense of humor to accomplish a lot!

Tip #13

They are self-confident

WOW *Idea #29*

Don't be afraid to make a judgment call.

What this refers to is not waiting for direction at every step. No high-level leader has time to hold their assistant's hand through every step of a new process. But many assistants are so afraid of making a mistake (sometimes the leader's fault due to the way they react to mistakes) that they are rendered unable to act until they get further direction from their leader.

There are certain things for which you will need to get direction. But as an executive assistant, you are expected to function like a leader and run with that direction without needing to check in on every little detail.

Analyze what is within your authority. Ask permission up front to run with certain decisions if it's unclear whether they are within your authority. If necessary, ask your leader to communicate to others that you have the authority and their backing to do this project. This will help you gain buy-in if others question your authority.

But if you carefully consider what you can and should do (or not), take responsibility for any mistakes that are made and look for guidance for the future, you can demonstrate to yourself and your leader how you can both incorporate more responsibilities into your job and advance your career.

Tip #13 (Continued)

They are self-confident

WOW *Idea #30*

Own up to your mistakes.

When you use your judgment, occasionally you will make a mistake. Hopefully, it won't be a fatal one, but rather a natural mistake that's to be expected of human beings.

Just own up to it as soon as you know about it, or if you can quickly correct it and relate the solution as well as the mistake, shortly thereafter.

One of the biggest fears of leaders is that people will make inevitable mistakes but then cover them up, or worse, blame them on someone else, which destroys team harmony.

So, own up to them and implement quick solutions, if possible. If that's not possible, at least develop the beginnings of a plan to solve them and present those plans at the time that you present the mistake. Never deny it. Most of the time they will find out anyway, and it will be worse if you've denied it up front.

Tip #13 (Continued)

They are self-confident

WOW *Idea #31*

Don't wait for permission to speak up in meetings.

Of course, this refers only to meetings where you're expected to participate, not meetings where you're simply present to take minutes or do other non-participant-related tasks.

But be an active, enthusiastic participant. Sitting there silently, waiting for people to call upon you before you speak, or even being hesitant when called upon does not display self-confidence.

When leaders are looking for people to advance or promote to higher positions, they will always look for those who have the self-confidence to lead themselves because those people are better candidates to lead others.

Tip #13 (Continued)

They are self-confident

WOW *Idea #32*

Speak up courageously when you have an idea or suggestion.

Another way to display self-confidence is to speak up when you observe something that should be changed, added or even eliminated.

We want to hear from you!

At one of my clients' companies, this comment, *"Speak up more courageously,"* actually appeared on a survey of managers who were asked what they wanted to see their assistants do. They also asked to have this topic included in the upcoming training session that I was conducting at their organization.

Great leaders want to hear from their people. They know they can't have all the good ideas to improve the organization. They also know that you have two advantages they don't have: a) you are on the front lines with all the other team members and know what they're saying, and b) you work with the systems and processes every day and know what works and what doesn't. So, your input is invaluable... and they realize it!

Tip #13 (Continued)

They are self-confident

WOW *Idea #33*

Sit next to the "power players" in the room during meetings.

Don't sit all the way at the back of the room, as far away from the leaders of the meeting as possible. You would never see a leader slink in and take a seat way in the back. Don't mistake sitting up front for being loud and calling attention to yourself. Many leaders lead quietly, but they are still leading – a term which implies being at the forefront, not bringing up the rear. If you want to lead, you must be up front.

I'm assuming that you either are a leader or desire to be one if you are reading this book; if so, it is important to demonstrate your leadership capabilities and make your presence known by visibly being someone who can take the lead.

Tip #13 (Continued)

They are self-confident

WOW *Idea #34*

Firm up your handshake.

A handshake is a good indication of a person's confidence. I know that during our current times (with COVID-19 all around us), handshakes are becoming a thing of the past, at least for the moment. But I am sure they will return when we are past this pandemic. In many countries, they are the most professional way for businesspeople to greet each other. In others, you would follow the customs there, but you would always make whatever that greeting is the most professional, respectful and confident it can be.

I still find far too many people (especially women) who have a weak, wimpy handshake. They either present two fingers for someone to shake (what is *that* all about?) or sometimes present their hand knuckles-forward, as if the other person is expected to kiss their ring! Even a full handshake is not self-confident if you barely grasp the hand you're shaking.

Don't be over-confident or arrogant and give someone a bone-crusher, either! That also says a lot about your personality and self-confidence, either displaying overconfidence or an incredible lack of self-confidence that you're trying to mask by overcompensating with your handshake.

The fist bump, elbow bump, wave or other no-contact gesture is fine for now – or among friends – but that "cutesy stuff" still doesn't fly with most people in the professional world.

Individual circumstances and customs will determine whether you go further and pull the person toward you, add a brief hug or offer a peck on one or both cheeks.

But for the most part, a professional handshake between colleagues will simply be one that is extended with your hand to the side, grasping the other hand firmly but not harshly and then releasing after a couple of seconds.

Tip #14

They realize that if their leader's schedule isn't 9-5, theirs isn't, either

WOW *Idea #35*

Let your leader know that if they're traveling and run into problems, they can call you at home any time in an emergency.

Don't make them wonder if it's OK to bother you at home or at odd hours in these cases. And don't make them feel guilty about doing so. There are many ways they can compensate you for being this flexible, but part of your job is ensuring the safety of your leader when in difficult or uncertain circumstances. In those instances, it's very reassuring for your leader to know they have someone they know and trust to help them.

Better you should be awakened at 2AM and can help your leader out of a difficult situation than for them to be stranded without resources, with a possible language barrier and without anyone they trust to whom they can turn.

I so appreciate you!

A situation like this arose for me while I was traveling in California. I was driving from the airport to a speaking location that should have been two hours away. I should have arrived by 7PM, but after I got on the road, I realized that something had happened and I wasn't going to arrive at the hotel until around midnight… and maybe not even then. I had a keynote early in the morning and wasn't sure how I was going to get there and try to get any sleep!

So, at 7PM (PT), I called my assistant, Patti, on the East Coast, which was 10PM for her. I needed her to call the hotel to be sure they didn't give away my room, and because the traffic was ridiculously heavy, I couldn't take my eyes of the road to try to find the number of the hotel so I could make the call myself.

I also wanted her to check to see if there were any other airports in between me and my destination that I could possibly get to and fly there.

I couldn't have done any of this on my own and still reached my destination. But Patti has made it clear that she will always be there for me. This situation was no different; she made all the phone calls I needed and called me back with the information she discovered.

I can't tell you what a treasure she is, especially at times when I just need someone I can trust to help me.

Thank you, Patti!

Tip #15

They truly enjoy what they do

WOW *Idea #36*

Don't let your work (or certain portions of it) visibly pile up on your desk.

When you don't enjoy doing something, it shows. We all have certain aspects of our jobs that we don't particularly enjoy. And we often procrastinate until the last possible moment to do them.

If this is the case with you, that's fine. But don't let it be evident. Don't let those files pile up on your desk if you hate filing. Conceal them somehow, so no one can pass by your desk and say, *"WOW, hate filing, do you?"*

People are always watching what you do. They notice things – and yes, sometimes even make things up! Don't give them any ammunition to make anything up or make it worse than it really is.

Let your enthusiasm show for the portions of your work that you love… and conceal well evidence of the portions you don't love.

This will serve you well in any leadership role you accept.

Chapter Three:

Call To Action

[3]

Call To Action

You can see by now, I'm sure, that this book contains many tips and ideas that can help you succeed.

Take them to heart. Review each one and look for creative ways to implement them into your position.

The new vision for your career should be as an **executive strategic partner** for your leader. That partner needs to be the absolute best they can be in order to help the leader, and the entire team, succeed.

Don't just put this book aside and do nothing different than you did before. If you put the ideas and tips contained here into action, the time and effort you expended to reach this point will pay off for yourself and your leader.

On the next page, you will find a brief Action Plan to help you answer some important questions about your goals, why they are important to you and who can help you achieve them. There is also a section for you to identify and list the top three actions you will take in the next seven days, along with estimated completion dates, to start your journey toward the goal of being an Invaluable Assistant and partner.

Three Steps, No Fail

One of my speaking colleagues once told me of a formula her uncle shared with her. It's called Three Steps, No Fail. If you identify three steps you can take in the next seven days, at which you cannot possibly fail, the next three steps will then be revealed to you. Repeat this process every seven days until you reach your goal. The formula is intended to help you build a bridge from where you are now to where you want to go.

My colleague is a singer as well as a speaker, and she followed this formula when she wanted to sell 100,000 CDs of her songs in Nashville, TN. Her first step was to buy a book about making it in the music business. Her second step was to call a voice teacher to see how much lessons would cost. The third was to order cable television so she could watch The Nashville Network. As you can see, all of these goals were simple enough that there was no way she could fail.

Once she completed the first three, she identified the three she would tackle the next week and the next and the next… and within a year, she reached her goal of selling 100,000 CDs of her songs in competitive Nashville, TN!

You can follow this formula, too. Identify three small things you can accomplish in the next seven days to help you reach your goal of serving your leader and your organization at a higher level.

And three steps at a time, you will achieve your new vision of moving from being merely indispensable to being truly invaluable.

Enjoy your journey!

Action Plan

What do I need to START doing to be an invaluable executive partner?

_____

What do I need to STOP doing to be an invaluable executive partner?

_____

What do I need to CONTINUE doing to be an invaluable executive partner?

_____

What skills, knowledge or training do I need to acquire?

_____

What assistance do I need to accomplish this training?

_____

Who can help me?

_____

My first step will be to: **Expected Completion Date**

_____

My second step will be to: **Expected Completion Date**

_____

My third step will be to: **Expected Completion Date**

_____

A QUICK FAVOR, PLEASE?

If you liked this book, please go to **Amazon.com** and leave an honest review. I love to hear from my readers and good reviews will help my book rank higher, which means that more people will see it and be able to benefit from its message.

My mission is to help empower every administrative professional to be the best executive partner they can be, and in the process receive as much joy and personal satisfaction as possible from their chosen career.

This will create a "domino effect" of success and turn every successful administrative professional into a positive role model of what is possible for others to achieve.

A FREE GIFT FOR YOU!

Because you've purchased Sandy's book, she'd like to offer you a free gift!

If you'd like a Cheat Sheet of all the tips and ideas contained in this book, please visit https://creatingthewow.com/ap-free-gift, enter your name and email address (don't worry, we will NEVER spam you or share your information with anyone!), and you'll receive an instant download link.

About Sandy Geroux, M.S.

Sandy Geroux, M.S., is a recognized expert on creating WOW experiences for customers and associates alike. Her programs focus on the impact of everyday, consistent actions that add up to exceptional experiences for everyone around us.

Since the year 2000, she has spoken to diverse audiences, helping leaders at every level inspire associates and co-workers to eliminate excuses, share their ideas and knowledge and go the extra mile to find the *hidden* WOWs that foster higher levels of customer service and employee engagement.

She is also a former administrative professional with over 20 years of experience. In addition, she has been conducting speaking, training and coaching engagement for this professional for 20 years, so she knows their challenges and joys. As a result, she is a passionate advocate for creating higher levels of performance and respect for the entire administrative profession.

She currently resides in Florida with her husband of 38 years.

For More Information or to book Sandy for a Speaking, Training or Coaching Consultation

Sandy's website address is:
www.theWOWplace.com

Or you can call or e-mail her at:
(407) 856-1188 / sandy@theWOWplace.com)

~

Sandy also has many free resources, including:

Sandy's blog containing quick tips on creating WOW experiences. She'd love for you to subscribe and comment on her posts any time you wish to share your WOW insights with others:

www.WOWplace.com

~

Social Media

Sandy's FaceBook page, containing program updates, great comments, and more links to information Sandy loves to share information that inspires others:

www.FaceBook.com/wowplace

~

Sandy is also on:
Twitter (@SandyGeroux)
LinkedIn
YouTube

Made in the USA
Monee, IL
05 March 2021